Fair Isle

through the seasons

Malachy Tallack and
Roger Riddington

Photographs by
Dave Wheeler
Mark Breaks
Deryk Shaw
Rebecca Nason
David Gifford
and others

Fair Isle: through the seasons
Published in 2010 by Z.E.Press

Copyright © Malachy Tallack and Roger Riddington, 2010.
Copyright for each photograph belongs to its photographer.

Designed by Malachy Tallack
Edited by Malachy Tallack and Roger Riddington
Printed by Crowes, Norfolk
ISBN: 978 0 9565526 0 0

Proceeds from the sale of this book will go to
Fair Isle Bird Observatory and the Fair Isle Community Association

This book would not have been possible without the skill and generosity of all the photographers, particularly Dave Wheeler, who responded to a stream of requests for images, old and new. Thanks also to Rob Duncan, Paul Harvey, Martin Heubeck, James McCallum, Fiona and Robert Mitchell, Andrew Morrison, Mike Pennington, Hollie and Deryk Shaw, Anne Sinclair, Rory Tallack, Brian Wilson and Dunrossness Community Council.

Contents

Introduction

There are many ways to see Fair Isle. For some, the island is a place of refuge – a haven – where it is possible to escape, for a time, the frantic disorder of the outside world. Here, visitors can find an uncommon peacefulness. There are no city sounds and no traffic jams; there is no crime. It is far away from what many long to escape. The island's remoteness, its quietude and calm, are, for these people, its greatest assets.

For others though, Fair Isle is an ornithological Mecca, where rare, migratory species can be seen on a uniquely regular basis, and where seabirds gather in great numbers to breed. Since the beginning of the twentieth century it has been a dream destination among birders from Britain and beyond. In spectacular scenery, and among friends and peers with shared passions, these visitors can indulge in some of the most exciting birdwatching the country has to offer, with the chance of something completely unexpected, always just a moment away.

For George Waterston, Fair Isle was a dream of freedom. For though he had already begun to make plans for the island after his first visit, several years earlier, it was during his time as a prisoner of war in the 1940s that he truly began to focus his thoughts upon the place. Inside the camp, far from home, Waterston worked furiously and in great detail, formulating his plans for a bird observatory and hostel. He developed scale drawings for the new building, estimated annual income and expenditure, and even created possible menus for the guests. He also tried to imagine how the island's fragile economy might be revived, and how the population, which by that time had fallen perilously low, could be prevented from collapsing completely. In these plans, Waterston found hope in an uncertain future.

For a few people, Fair Isle is home – a place of comfort and hard work, of community and belonging. The population today is around 70, and has remained quite stable for many years. Much has changed here in the past few decades. The island is less isolated, more connected than ever before; the modern world has made its way into every home and workplace. But much, still, remains the same. There is a rhythm to island life that is almost unchanged. The turning of the seasons still dictates the work of crofters, the comings and goings of visitors, the bird migrations of spring and autumn, and the weather – the inescapable weather.

This book, I hope, will reveal something of that rhythm, and something, too, of that life.

For more than 60 years, Fair Isle's community and its observatory have existed not as two separate entities, but as pieces of the same whole. Each is part of the other, and both are infinitely richer for that union. The opening, in 2010, of a brand new observatory, is testament to the success that it continues to enjoy, and that it shares with the island. It is testament also to a great deal of hope.

While a prisoner of war, George Waterston dreamed that Fair Isle 'could be restored to a happy thriving community where the young people would feel assured of a definite future living on the island.' No visitor can fail to appreciate the hard work and resilience that has been required to make this dream a reality, or the supreme achievement that it is, indeed, a reality.

This book celebrates that achievement. It celebrates the success of the observatory and of the community. It celebrates this island's beauty and its diversity. And it demonstrates, I hope, that there are many ways to see Fair Isle.

Malachy Tallack

Spring

After a long winter, spring is always the most welcome of seasons, bringing warmth and new life to the island. There is much work to be done though, with the arrival of lambs and a return to ploughing and planting. Spring also brings the first migrant birds of the year to the island, and sees breeding seabirds returning to the cliffs.

Above: The Kirk, built in the late nineteenth century.

Left: Fair Isle emerges from the morning mist, with the island's two wind-turbines just visible. The 60MW aero-generator on The Houll was erected in 1982, and was the first commercial wind power project in Europe. Both turbines are owned and maintained by Fair Isle Electricity Company, of which islanders are the only shareholders.

At Kirkigeo, a row of sheltered 'noosts' can be seen, where boats have traditionally been drawn up to protect them from the sea. Though far fewer are now occupied than was once the case (see above left), Kirkigeo is still used for the purpose. The Fair Isle yoal, as seen here, is a more streamlined relative of the Ness yoal, from mainland Shetland. It is a clinker-built vessel and has its roots in the boats used by the Norsemen. Yoals are still built on the island today by Ian Best, who was trained as a boat-builder in Norway.

There is a large breeding population of Northern Wheatears in Fair Isle during the summer months, but the species is also a common spring migrant. These migrants include birds of the larger, brighter, Greenland race, en-route to the far north.

The start of lambing in April truly marks the beginning of a new season in Fair Isle.

The 'Hill Road' winds its way up towards the communications mast on Ward Hill.

Fair Isle has long been renowned for its distinctive style of knitwear, consisting of geometric patterns in rows, with only two colours per row. At one time, islanders produced large quantities of knitted goods for barter and sale; it was an essential industry. The wool would be spun from island sheep, and then dyed at home, often in bright colours. Though recognised worldwide, Fair Isle cannot copyright its own name, so clothing created in any country can be sold as 'Fair Isle knitwear'. In 1980, a crafts co-operative was formed on the island to help market the goods and supply necessary tools and materials to knitters. It has provided part-time employment to many people over the years. Today, authentic island knitwear can still be purchased from Fair Isle Crafts.

Left: The Heligoland trap at 'the Plantation'. This motley collection of stunted trees along the Vaadal stream dates back to the 1950s, since when it has been a reliable magnet for tired migrants.

Above left: Shetland Starlings are the commonest landbird breeding in Fair Isle, and have proved a convenient study organism for generations of research students. The subspecies *zetlandicus*, which occurs throughout Shetland, including Fair Isle, is generally thought to be separable from those elsewhere in Scotland. Fair Isle has its very own Wren, however (above right), which rejoices in the magnificent scientific name of *Troglodytes troglodytes fridariensis*. Some 25–40 pairs of this endemic form are present, nesting chiefly along the island's coastline.

Stackhoull Stores, Fair Isle's shop and Post Office, is a vital service. The shop is extremely well stocked with food and household goods, and on a Wednesday morning, when fresh fruit and vegetables are on the shelves, it can be a very busy place. The shop is also an important social hub, where island news can be heard and passed on. Almost as much talking as shopping is done there at times.

During spring and autumn, the routine of recording the migrant birds passing through Fair Isle has changed little since the observatory was first established. The daily census (left) is carried out every morning, weather permitting; the island is divided into three, with an observer covering a similar route in each sector and counting all species. Birds caught in the Heligoland traps allow more detailed information, such as size, weight, age, sex and body condition, to be measured. All the birds trapped are fitted with a tiny, uniquely coded ring, which provides a means to understand more about movements, longevity and other aspects of their life history if they are caught or found again at a later date.

Ploughing in Fair Isle: Willie Eunson with Bella and John Irvine in 1936 (above); Jerry Stout in 1980 (below left); Iain Stout in 2005 (right).

Fulmars patrol the west cliffs, with the crofts of the south lying beyond.

Dazzling breeding plumage compensates for the fact that the numbers of migrants seen in spring tends to be lower, and less predictable, than in autumn. Red-backed Shrike (top), Rustic Bunting (bottom) and Bluethroat (right) are scarce but regular visitors in May and early June.

Fair Isle Primary School is at the very heart of the community.

Fulmars (opposite) are remarkably successful seabirds, now the commonest bird nesting in Fair Isle – yet little more than a century ago they had yet to colonise the island. Kittiwakes (above left) symbolise the declining Fair Isle seabird populations of the past two decades. Almost 20,000 pairs bred on the island in 1988, but numbers are now less than a quarter of that total, and birds like this one, perched on a former nest site, have all too frequently struggled to raise young in recent years. Guillemots (above right) are one of the most sociable of seabirds, and the noise and the activity of their densely packed colonies is endlessly fascinating during spring and early summer.

A brief history of
island ornithology

In the decades before the establishment of the bird observatory, ornithological studies in Fair Isle developed through the twin axes of some distinguished visiting ornithologists and a number of skilled and diligent islanders.

Dr William Eagle Clarke.

The discovery of Fair Isle as one of the great bird migration crossroads of Europe was made by **Dr William Eagle Clarke**, who first visited the island in autumn 1905. Clarke was a museum ornithologist (he became curator at the Royal Scottish Museum in 1906) but in Fair Isle he found a place that could rival the German island of Helgoland for bird migration studies. He returned almost annually until the outbreak of World War I, but also trained islanders to carry out observations and recording in his absence. The first of these was **George Wilson Stout** of Busta (who left the island in 1909, and was later killed in the first war), followed by **Jerome Wilson** of Springfield. Clarke and his co-workers, chiefly these two, added 35 species to the Shetland list in the first ten years of study in Fair Isle, as well as six species new to Britain.

Other notable ornithologists to visit the island in those early years included **Norman Boyd Kinnear** (who accompanied Clarke on his first trip and was later one of the first trustees of the observatory) and **Mary du Caurroy Tribe, Duchess of Bedford**, who made nine visits between 1909 and 1914.

Eagle Clarke last visited Fair Isle in 1921, and on that trip brought his successor, **Surgeon Rear Admiral John Hutton Stenhouse**. An enthusiastic collector and recorder during his naval career, Stenhouse was encouraged by Clarke to make a series of expeditions to Fair Isle, seven in total, between 1921 and 1927. Stenhouse also realised the potential of the island men for recording migration, and developed his own protégé, **George Stout** of Field, generally known simply as 'Fieldy'. Indeed, for a large part of the inter-war years, at least after Stenhouse's final visit, Fair Isle ornithology was largely in the hands of Fieldy and Jerome Wilson.

Surgeon Rear Admiral John Hutton Stenhouse.

From left: George Waterston, George 'Fieldy' Stout, James A. Stout.

The first warden of Fair Isle was **Ken Williamson**, who remained in post for eight years. Since 1948, the monitoring of bird migration has continued every spring and autumn, using a more or less similar methodology, supervised by the warden (and usually helped by between one and three assistant wardens, although the first dedicated 'AW', **Valerie Thom**, was not appointed until 1955). However, the tradition of interest and involvement in bird recording by the islanders has also continued and particular mention should be made of both **Jimmy Wilson** of Schoolton ('School Jimmy'), who was the son of Jerome Wilson, and **James A. Stout** of Midway ('Mires Jimmy'), the son of Fieldy. Both of these men were skilled and accurate observers, who contributed much to the ornithology of the island without getting the recognition they perhaps deserved.

Jimmy Wilson ('School Jimmy').

George Waterston, one of the great pioneers of Scottish ornithology in the middle years of the twentieth century, met Stenhouse at the Royal Scottish Museum and learned of the Fair Isle studies initiated by Eagle Clarke. Waterston's first trip to Fair Isle was in 1935, when the idea of a permanent bird observatory was firmly established. Waterston made several visits in the years before the outbreak of World War II and developed a close relationship with George Stout, often staying with him at Field. The war interrupted progress but Waterston eventually bought the island in 1948 (for £3,500), and the bird observatory opened in August that year.

Migration continues to be one of the key themes of the ornithological work at the observatory, although monitoring the island's important seabird populations has assumed an increasing importance since the 1980s. In addition, academic researchers are also now a regular part of the ornithological scene, typically working either on seabirds or, particularly, the abundant island population of Starlings.

Summer

Summer is a time of light – of long days and short nights. The cliffs are clamorous with seabirds and their chicks: Fulmars, Gannets, Guillemots, and many others, making the most of this all-too-brief season. Everywhere the island feels full of life, and the long hours of the 'simmer dim', when the bright glow of the evening sun stretches long past midnight, can be intoxicating for both visitors and locals alike.

Sea Pinks adorn the banks.

Setting lobster creels close to shore.

Puffins would probably win any popular vote for 'favourite seabird' and these small but charismatic members of the auk family are common around Fair Isle's coast. Many birds at the colony at Roskilie, near the observatory, are fitted with lightweight plastic colour bands, allowing individuals to be recognised from year to year and survival rates to be monitored.

As with all of Fair Isle's seabirds, Puffin breeding success is heavily dependent on food supply and the photo on the right encapsulates the difference between success and failure. The bird on the left has a full load of small sandeels (and a single large gadoid). Small, oil-rich shoaling fish, but particularly sandeels, are high in energy and ideal for chick growth. In contrast, the pipefish carried by the other bird is low in energy and difficult to swallow. The scarcity of sandeels in particular has been a key factor in the population declines of Shetland's seabirds during the 2000s.

One of the definitive landmarks of Fair Isle is Sheep Rock, connected to the main island by a low, inaccessible land bridge. As its name implies, the rock was formerly used for grazing sheep, and was considered to be among the best land for the purpose. Islanders made the perilous climb up the eastern side of the rock in order to reach the animals, which could then be lowered on ropes to the waiting boats below. The last sheep were taken off in the 1980s.

Arctic Terns are one of the champion travellers of the bird world, breeding in the far north, and wintering in the southern oceans, as far as the Antarctic pack ice. Arctic Terns have nested in Fair Isle in markedly fluctuating numbers in recent years, probably in response to the availability of sandeels. Numbers peaked at over 2,800 pairs in 2001, yet only 115 pairs bred the following year.

Gannets are the largest and perhaps most successful of Fair Isle's seabirds. They colonised the island only recently, with the first successful pairs nesting on Dronger in 1975. Since then, numbers have increased almost every year. Gannets can feed on a wide variety of fish species, including larger prey unavailable to smaller seabirds, while their size enables them to undertake long-range foraging trips. These factors make them less vulnerable to local fluctuations in fish stocks.

Fair Isle lichens and mosses.

To the Glory of God
in Remembrance of Agnes Stout
Beloved Wife of Jerome Stout.

Awaiting the Going Down
of the Sun
to be Joined Again in Paradise.

41

In the past, islanders had to make many of the things they needed, so craft skills were passed down through the generations. Some of these skills have continued to be practised here, alongside other, less traditional crafts.

Opposite page (left): Inside the kirk are two stained-glass windows created in memory of Agnes Stout by Patrick Ross-Smith.

Opposite page (right): Straw-backed chairs have long been made in Fair Isle, and Stewart Thomson of Quoy has continued this tradition, using oats grown on the island.

This page: Stewart Thomson of Shirva has built over 100 spinning wheels. This wheel was made of wood salvaged from the old observatory buildings.

The Oysterplant is a rare, northern species that grows on a very few sandy or shingly beaches in Shetland. The specimens at Muckle Uri Geo have thrived in recent years, protected from grazing sheep. In summer the plant is an impressive sight, studded with brilliant blue flowers.

Cottongrass, or Bog Cotton, blooms in thick carpets over some of the marshier parts of the island in summer, such as Da Water and Boini Mire.

For many years, groups of volunteers, organised by the National Trust for Scotland and the International Voluntary Service, have visited Fair Isle in summer to help with crofting work and other tasks. They work alongside islanders for two weeks, and in that time experience something of island life. At the end of their stay, the groups will often organise a barbeque at the Puffinn hostel, to which everyone will be invited. The social aspect of the workcamps is hugely important, and some volunteers return year after year, and make lasting friendships within the community.

Opposite: Many yachts visit during the summer, and at times the North Haven can become surprisingly crowded.

Great Skuas, or Bonxies, are perhaps the most controversial birds in Shetland. A significant proportion (over 40%) of the total world population nests in Shetland, with over 200 pairs in Fair Isle. They are, however, brutally efficient predators, and have had an undeniable impact on the populations of other seabirds in the islands.

Bonxies are adept at defending their nests and young against human intruders (above), while their characteristic display (below) is a feature of their breeding territories on the hill.

The Arctic Skua, closely related to the Bonxie, is equally intimidating when defending its nest.

For the staff at the bird observatory, the summer months are dominated by the island's breeding seabirds. The observatory has been part of a national programme of seabird monitoring since 1986. Much of the work involves recording population levels and breeding success. But some work is more 'hands on', and visits to seabird colonies to ring chicks and adults, measure growth rates and the body condition of chicks, and collect food samples, are a key part of the programme. A head for heights is essential to reach some of the colonies (shown here is the descent into the Gannet colony at Guidicum). Handling an adult Puffin (the one above is being fitted with colour rings – see p33) requires extreme care and attention; as well as a powerful bill, their strong feet have sharp claws that can lacerate hands in an instant.

Looking over the Auld Haa and Skerryholm, towards the South Harbour, Utra and the South Lighthouse.

The hill sheep, of which each croft owns a share, are gathered every summer to be sheared. The roundup requires many hands (and paws).

While most crofting jobs today can be done alone, baling silage still requires many hands. Neighbours help with cutting, lifting and wrapping bales on each croft, and the help is reciprocated. The children also get involved with the activities.

The cliffs along Fair Isle's west coast offer spectacular views for walkers, such as here, looking north from Malcolm's Head.

The *Good Shepherd IV* is more than just a ferry; It is crucial to every-day life on the island. Not only does it bring tourists and islanders back and forth from Shetland, the boat carries all goods to be sold in Stackhoull Stores, it brings building materials, animal feed, mail and vehicles (right), takes the island's waste out for disposal, and ships livestock out to market in the autumn. In addition, the ferry also provides good jobs and steady incomes for several families. It is a lifeline for Fair Isle in a myriad of ways. The current vessel is the fourth *Good Shepherd*, and came into service in 1986. She was purpose-built for the job. Though the ferry has a somewhat less-than-positive reputation among passengers prone to seasickness, she was considered a great improvement on the previous boat. The crossing time between Fair Isle and Grutness is two and a half hours, and the ferry sails three times a week in summer.

Each year, in summer, around a dozen cruise ships visit Fair Isle. Passengers come ashore to explore the island, to see Puffins and other seabirds on the cliffs, and to enjoy local crafts and knitwear, displayed in the community hall.

Above is the *Hebridean Princess*, a regular visitor. Left, cruise passengers step up onto the old slipway in the North Haven.

A brief history of
the Fair Isle community

Fair Isle's first human inhabitants arrived more than six thousand years ago. They came in boats of wood and animal hide, from Scotland, through the islands of Orkney, and then onwards to Shetland. At each stage, they were drawn on by the promise of new land on the horizon ahead.

Whether these Mesolithic people settled or moved back and forth as nomads among the islands is uncertain, but there was food here for

Landberg, site of an Iron Age fort excavated in the late 1990s.

the taking – fish, shellfish, birds and sea mammals – and permanent populations were resident in Shetland well before 3000BC. Concurrent to this was the development of a kind of primitive farming, which, as it developed, would define Shetlanders' relationship with their place for millennia to come.

In Fair Isle, evidence for these first settlers is minimal, and may well have been lost to rising seas and coastal erosion, but there is a wealth of archaeological material left by later peoples. These include late-Neolithic land divisions, or 'dykes', numerous Bronze Age 'burnt mounds', such as at Setter (the largest example in Shetland), and the Iron Age fort at Landberg.

Fair Isle's first appearance in written history came much later, after the original inhabitants had been displaced by Vikings and the Norse settlers that followed them. For the Norsemen, the island was Friðarey, and it features prominently in the *Orkneyinga Saga*, which was written about 1200AD, and records events that took place three centuries earlier. The vast majority of Fair Isle's place names have their origins in this period, which lasted officially until 1469, when the island, along with the rest of Shetland, was pawned in lieu of a dowry payment by King Christian I of Denmark and Norway to King James III of Scotland. They were never returned.

Unofficially, allegiances and connections to Norway remained for a considerable time, and were probably strengthened by the poor conditions suffered by islanders. Scottish lairds, who in some instances ruled the isles like despots, helped to ensure that living standards for most Shetlanders were rarely much higher than bare survival.

By the eighteenth century, life was still extraordinarily hard for Fair Islanders. Crofting provided for only the most basic needs, and fishing was a necessity. Some men also went to work at the Greenland whale fishery during the summer months, earning more there than they could hope to at home.

During this period, the population of the island, though always vulnerable to diseases such as smallpox, grew rapidly, and by the mid-nineteenth century it had reached unsustainable levels. In 1861, there were 380 people living on the island, and despite a gradual overflow of families, relocating mostly to Orkney, a more drastic event was inevitable.

That event took place the following year, when a sloop called the *No Joke* carried 137 emigrants from Fair Isle to Kirkwall. From there, the islanders travelled across the Atlantic to Saint John, New Brunswick. This was the beginning of a steady depopulation, through voluntary emigration and occasional evictions by landowners. At the turn of the twentieth century, 147 people lived on the island, and by the 1960s it was just 46. In 100 years, the population had gone from unsustainably high to unsustainably low. Many believed that total depopulation was inevitable, and for a time the shadow of St Kilda, entirely emptied of people, lay upon the island.

The transferral of Fair Isle's ownership, from the Bruce estate to George Waterston in 1948, and from Waterston to the National Trust for Scotland in 1954, marked the beginning of a new chapter in the island's history. The National Trust, in partnership with the community, set in motion the social improvements that would eventually halt

Inside Fair Isle's museum, the George Waterston Memorial Centre.

the island's decline. Modernisation of housing was the principle concern, and over the next two decades major building improvements were made, along with the provision of electricity and running water for every house. Much of the work was done by islanders themselves, with the help of work camp volunteers.

Over the years there have been many changes – some significant, others subtle – that have contributed to building the strong community that visitors will find in Fair Isle today: a community standing firmly on its own feet, looking forward.

Autumn

For crofters, autumn brings the rewards of a year's hard work. Vegetables are harvested and animals are sold at market; this is the climax of the agricultural year. And as the weather begins to turn, and cold sharpens the air, autumn is often the climax of the ornithological year, with the possibility of the next rare migrant always just on the horizon.

There were once more than half a dozen 'click mills' on the Gilsetter Burn, used for grinding grain from the island's crofts, but the last of these ceased to be used in the early part of the twentieth century. Today only the shells of a few mills remain, at the head of the Gill of Finniquoy, along with numerous millstones set into the earth (above).

'The Gully' trap, straddling the Gilsetter burn, may look careworn but this is unquestionably one of the finest Heligoland traps anywhere in Europe (right). This type of trap, first developed on the German island of Helgoland, is the main method of catching small migrant birds on Fair Isle. There are around ten permanent traps on the island, but it is the Gully trap (plans for which were first discussed by George Waterston after his visit in 1935) that ringers most look forward to checking on the first round of an autumn day.

Fair Isle is renowned for attracting rare eastern vagrants in autumn. The four species shown here have become known as 'Fair Isle specials' because of the high proportion of all British records that involve birds seen in Fair Isle. Yellow-breasted Buntings (left, Springfield, September 1997) are typically found in the vicinity of standing oat crops. The Lanceolated Warbler (top, Upper Stoneybrek, September 2007) is perhaps the quintessential 'little brown job'; as with Pallas's Grasshopper Warblers (bottom, Haa, October 2008), more than 80% of British records are from Shetland, and predominantly Fair Isle. The 'zebra-striped' Pechora Pipit (right, Quoy, September 2006) completes the quartet.

There are considerably fewer crops grown on the island today than in times past. Fields of oats were once a common sight in the autumn, but now very little is grown, and silage, which is more reliable and less labour-intensive, has replaced hay as the principal sheep fodder.

An impressive array of tractors gathered at the hill crü (sheep pen).

In autumn, lambs that have been reared on the island are transported to mainland Shetland to be sold at the livestock marts in Lerwick.

Autumn migration is eagerly anticipated by birdwatchers in Fair Isle. Large flocks of thrushes such as Redwings (above) are a feature of October days with easterly winds, which may also bring Yellow-browed Warblers (below) and Common Redpolls (right).

As well as birds, there are many other elements to the natural history interest of Fair Isle. Although most cetacean sightings come from the crew and passengers aboard the *Good Shepherd*, Orcas (or Killer Whales) are seen occasionally in the summer months, close to the island's shoreline where they hunt for fish or seals. More than any other creature these are guaranteed to cause a stir among islanders and visitors alike.

Fair Isle has a healthy population of Grey Seals, and around 60–100 pups are born each autumn on the inaccessible beaches of the island's north and west coasts, mainly during October.

The south end of the isle in autumn light. Clockwise from top left: Burkle, with Kenaby beyond; Koolin and Springfield; Midway, with Shirva beyond; looking northeast towards Sheep Rock from Utra croft. Opposite page: Looking northwest from Meoness.

Fair Isle's reputation for rare migrants is legendary, but it is the 'firsts' – species new to Britain – that people remember most. Left, Britain's first Siberian Rubythroat was found near the Plantation in 1975 (this one, the third for Fair Isle and fifth for Britain, was photographed on the island in October 2005). Top, the Rufous-tailed Robin of October 2004 is still the only British record. Bottom, Brown Flycatcher was first recorded in July 1992, although this one, the third for Britain, was seen in October 2008.

A first for Britain brings unprecedented numbers of travelling birders, or twitchers, to Fair Isle – and traffic on the island's airstrip. Above, just some of those who travelled to see the Citril Finch in June 2008. Below, the scene in October 2003, when two exceptional rarities – a Siberian Rubythroat and Savannah Sparrow, from North America – brought a record count of charter planes.

Fair Isle has two lighthouses – one in the north and one in the south. The North Light (shown here) covers the water between Fair Isle and Shetland, a very dangerous stretch of sea. Prior to their construction a great many ships were lost on the rocks around the island. Most famous among these was *El Gran Griffon*, part of the Spanish Armada, which went aground at Stroms Heelor in September 1588. On that occasion, the ship's 300 crewmen managed to get ashore safely, but over the years many other sailors were not so lucky. The South Light was illuminated for the first time in January 1892, and the North Light began work in November of the same year. Both were designed by David and Charles Stevenson, cousins of the writer Robert Louis Stevenson and part of the renowned family of lighthouse engineers. The buildings are noticably different in size; the tower at the south is 26 metres high, while that at the north is just 14, though it sits atop 60 metre cliffs, so is well elevated above sea level. Both lighthouses also had fog horns (above left) for warning ships at times of poor visibility, but these are no longer used. For much of the twentieth century, three keepers and their families lived at each lighthouse, but in 1983 the North Light was automated, with engineers at the south providing cover when needed. Then, 15 years later, the South Light too was automated. It was the last Scottish lighthouse to be manned.

A rain shower passes close by the island.

The South Light at sunset.

A brief history of
the observatory

George Waterston's vision for a bird observatory in Fair Isle was crystallised during his first visit to the island, in 1935. Almost 13 years later, his dreams finally became a reality as the observatory was opened on 28th August 1948. The former naval huts at the North Haven were adapted and these housed staff and visitors for over 20 years.

The naval huts housing the observatory in its year of opening, 1948.

Towards the end of the 1960s, with the need to replace the naval huts becoming ever more apparent, Waterston launched a public appeal for funds. A new, purpose-built observatory was duly opened at Mavers Cup, just above and to the south of the Havens, in autumn 1969. A timber building, prefabricated in Devon and brought in by boat from Berwick-upon-Tweed, it offered new levels of comfort for visitors, and became widely (and fondly) regarded as 'the birdwatchers' Hilton'.

The new building at Mavers Cup, 1969.

Eighteen years later, showing signs of wear and tear, the observatory underwent significant refurbishment during the winter of 1988/89. It was extended somewhat and the walls were encased in harled blockwork. Although this facelift extended the life of the building until 2009, problems with (in particular) the flat roof and the original plumbing system meant that a more radical solution was eventually necessary.

The refurbished observatory prior to demolition in 2009.

After considering both relocation and wholesale renovation, it was decided that the observatory would close for a season, the ailing buildings would be demolished and a new, energy-efficient version would be rebuilt on the same site. A major fundraising campaign was launched and, with the aid of substantial grants from the Scottish Government, Shetland Islands Council and Highlands & Islands Enterprise, plus smaller grants from many other sources and a successful public appeal, work commenced on schedule in spring 2009.

The old observatory was soon demolished and the site prepared, before sections of the building or 'pods' were brought in by barge from Orkney. The second 'new observatory' was duly opened in spring 2010.

Winter

Winter always seems to outstay its welcome. By the end of February, when strong winds and storms are still pounding the island, the warmth of summer can feel a very long way off indeed. But Fair Isle can be spectacular even in the worst of weathers, and homes are never more homely than when the wind and rain are beating at the windows. Winter is also when the social life of the island is most important.

'*So what do you do in the winter?*' Many visitors forget that, with only 70 residents, and a multitude of services and amenities to maintain, islanders are kept busy in every season. Most people have several part-time jobs, which might include coastguard duties (left), fire brigade (above) and roads maintenance (below).

Winter is a quiet time for birding. Greylag Geese, Snow Buntings and Ravens are staple fare.

There are several types of sheep in Fair Isle. On the hill land in the north of the island, there are only pure-bred Shetland sheep, such as these, but elsewhere on the crofts you will find other breeds, including pure and cross-bred Cheviots, Texels and Suffolks.

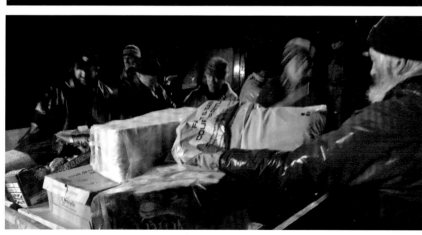

The *Good Shepherd IV* sails only once a week in winter, but help is needed when unloading the cargo, whatever the weather.

Fair Isle today is linked with the outside world to a degree that would have been unimaginable to previous generations. For half the year, seven flights a week are scheduled between the island's airstrip and Tingwall airport in Shetland's central mainland, with a further one flight from Sumburgh airport. During the winter months there are six weekly flights. The timetable, as well as giving visitors great flexibility, means islanders can take day trips when necessary, and allows children attending high school in Lerwick to return for weekends at home quite regularly. The real determiner of flight frequency in Fair Isle though is not the timetable but the weather, and occasionally the island is cut off entirely, with neither the plane nor the ferry able to make the journey. This enforced isolation can be one of the most difficult parts of living here, but islanders learn to accept it as an unavoidable fact of life.

Prolonged periods of heavy snow are quite unusual in the Northern Isles, but most winters bring occasional spells, and the island can be very quickly transfomed into a strange and beautiful landscape.

Shetland is world famous for its musical heritage, and Fair Isle is certainly no exception. The island has produced more than its fair share of outstanding musicians, such as Chris Stout (left) and Inge Thomson (right). Live music is a regular event at the bird observatory in summer, where visitors can hear local artists performing tunes and songs. During the winter there is still plenty of socialising going on, with dances in the hall at Christmas and New Year, and meals for the whole community, as well as regular events such as the weekly darts club and 'keep fit' group.

On the 17th January, 1941, a German Heinkel 111 aircraft crash landed at Vaasetter, killing two of its crew. Remarkably, the other three crew members all survived the impact, and were met by a small group of islanders, led by George 'Fieldy' Stout, who made a citizen's arrest. The pilot of the Heinkel, Karl Heinz Thurz, returned to the island in 1987 to revisit the scene. Both of the engines, plus a large section of the tail and fuselage, still lie at the site, and are some of the most complete German aircraft remains to be found above ground anywhere.

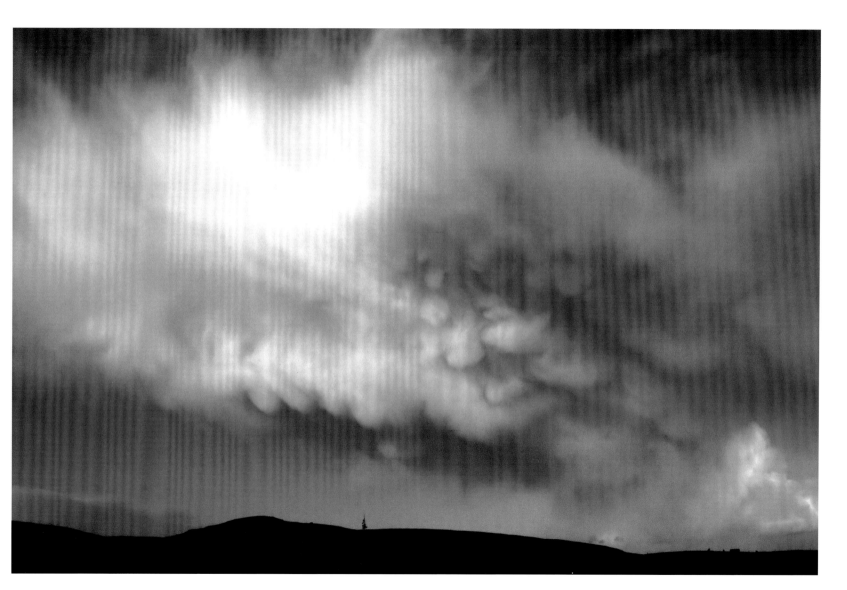

The tradition of 'guizing' has remained virtually unchanged for generations. On New Year's Eve, groups of islanders dress up in a variety of costumes and visit every house to perform a sketch. The occupants of the house must then try to guess who their mysterious visitors might be.

Credits

Malachy Tallack is a writer and singer-songwriter. He is editor of *Shetland Life* magazine and lived in Fair Isle from 2005 to 2009. *www.malachytallack.com*

Roger Riddington is editor of *British Birds* magazine and co-author of *Birds of Shetland*. He was warden of Fair Isle Bird Observatory from 1994 to 1997, and assistant warden in 1992.

Photographers

Dave Wheeler
www.davewheelerphotography.com

All photographs by Dave Wheeler except as detailed below.

Mark Breaks
www.breaksbirdphotography.co.uk

Pages 13, 22, 25, 33, 34, 38, 64, 65 (bottom), 73, 74 (top left), 77 (bottom), 90 (bottom left).

Deryk Shaw

Pages 18 (left), 32, 49, 58, 74 (bottom and right), 83 (bottom right), 84 (bottom right), 90 (top and bottom right).

Rebecca Nason
www.rebeccanason.com

Pages 14 (left), 17, 26, 37, 48, 65 (top), 77 (left and top).

David Gifford
www.davegifford.co.uk

Pages 6, 7 (bottom), 8, 11, 14 (right), 15, 80 (right), 92.

Tim Loseby, pages 47 (bottom), 65 (left); **Roger Riddington,** page 18 (right); **Nicola Breaks,** page 47 (top); **David Tipling**, page 54 (right); **Anne Sinclair**, page 60; **Paul Baxter,** page 65 (right); **James W. Stout**, page 107 (top row, middle).

Pages 20 (top), 27 (left), 28 (left) 83 (left and top) courtesy of F.I.B.O.T.; page 7 (top left) courtesy of George Waterston Memorial Centre; page 28 (right) courtesy of Brian Wilson. Page 27 (right), photographer unknown.